Still Small Moments © 2017 by April Dawn Best

All rights reserved. No part of this publication may be reproduced, distributed, or transmitted in any form or by any means, including photocopying, recording, or other electronic or mechanical methods, without the prior written permission of the publisher or author, except in the case of brief quotations embodied in critical reviews and certain other noncommercial uses permitted by copyright law. For permission requests, email the publisher or author at addresses below:

Contact the author:
www.aprildbest.com | twitter: @AprilDawnBest
aprildawnbest@gmail.com | instagram: still.small.moments

Contact the publisher:
Unprecedented Press LLC - 495 Sleepy Hollow Ln, Holland, MI 49423
www.unprecedentedpress.com | info@unprecedentedpress.com
twitter: @UnprecdntdPress | instagram: unprecedentedpress

Scripture quotations marked (ESV) are from the ESV® Bible (The Holy Bible, English Standard Version®), copyright © 2001 by Crossway, a publishing ministry of Good News Publishers. Used by permission. All rights reserved.

ISBN-10:0-9987602-2-6
ISBN-13:978-0-9987602-2-3

Printed in the United States of America
Ingram Printing & Distribution, 2017

Edited by Joshua Best
Designed & Illustrated by Lauren Moura

First Edition

Unprecedented
Press

still small moments

april dawn best

table of contents

Dedication	11
Introduction	13
1. the moment before the photo is taken	**17**
Real life isn't picture perfect	20
Memories of moments are framed by photos	23
The moments not pictured	27
Make room for the unexpected	32
2. capture the moment	**37**
Telescopic view	37
Microscopic view	41
Perspective paradox	46
3. faithful in the moment	**55**
Faithful in your field	55
Peace in the process	59
Miracle in the mundane	65
4. maximize the moment	**71**
Leaders in our sphere	71
Upward and downward growth	76
Upward growth	77
Downward growth	81

5. rest in the moment — 87

    A nest for herself — 87
    Sanity time — 89
    Beauty in the now — 91
    Keeping your tank full — 92

6. the power of the moment — 99

    Opportune timing with kids — 103
    Face time — 106

7. remember the moment — 111

    Real emotion — 113
    Still small moments — 117

    About The Author — 120
    Everyone Global Giving Fund — 121
    Other Titles — 122

This book is dedicated to my husband Josh whose love and encouragement pushed me to make this book a reality and to my kids who have taught me more more about myself, God, and life than I could ever imagine.

introduction

The heart behind this book grew from a desire to fully embrace every season of life without nostalgic regret for the past or hopeful desire for the future. I've spent most of my adult life planning for the future. In college, I planned for the next assignment, the next class, the next holiday. Teaching high school and middle school full-time, I worked for the future lesson plan, the future week, the future break. Getting my Master's Degree was all about moving towards the next project and achievement. My son was born as I finished that degree, and his birth began to shift the way I interacted with the present. It wasn't until he was two and a half years old and my daughter was six months old that I quit working part-time to be home with them. It was this transition that brought my attention to the fact that I spent most of my time unconsciously wishing the days away. It was a habit that needed to be changed. Coming to a place of peace and rest in the present moment regardless of its perfection or imperfection meant a change in thought and heart. This book chronicles some of the failures and lessons learned as this desire to seek the still small moments in life throughout all seasons in life. Certain small moments in life are massively transformative—God can powerfully change something in our lives in a moment. Other small moments are unimpressive and quiet. From the mundane to the majestic, there are opportunities for miracles everyday.

I pray you find grace and freedom on the pages of this book.

Sincerely,
April

1
the moment before the photo is taken

Expectations frame our whole world. The expectations we have about kids before having kids are laughable. Whether those expectations were wildly off base or mildly different from present reality, the way we perceive and interact with the moment we're in is affected by our expectations surrounding it.

Managing our expectations about parenting and what it really looks like frees us to embrace the moment we're in instead of creating falsely staged ones. Pinterest, Instagram, Facebook, and other social media platforms frame our expectations more than the day-to-day realties of parenting. I struggle with meeting these unrealistic expectations and unnecessary pressures. We run to grab our phones to capture every moment of joy and beauty and then spend the next 20 minutes trying to recreate that perfect instance. We throw our phones at the wall in frustration when everyday life does not live up to our expectations. Or we word vomit all our frustrations and send them out for all the world to see what real life parenting actually looks like.

The hardest thing about expectations is the weight we carry trying to meet them. We have expectations within ourselves that we're constantly negotiating in our own minds. We have expectations from friends and family we're navigating. When we fail to meet our own expectations, disappointment sets in. When we fail to meet other people's expectations, frustration and guilt or resentment build up.

Parenting is work. It's beautiful, exhausting, rewarding, frustrating, awe-inspiring work. When we embrace this truth, the good moments and the bad ones make sense.

When we have realistic expectations of ourselves and our kids, freedom comes and comparison ceases. It's impossible to have a conversation with another parent without talking about sleeping, eating, and milestones. There was one time when I overheard another mom talking with her friend about her baby's sleep. Our babies were just a few weeks apart and the closeness in age automatically set me up for comparison. She went on to share that for the past few weeks her baby was sleeping almost 12 hours straight through the night and was taking consistently long naps.

At six weeks old, my daughter, Edith, was in no way sleeping long stretches at night. She napped for long stretches only when being worn in a baby wrap. She had just spent the last week crying inconsolably between 7 pm and 11 pm. Nothing I could do or tried to do calmed her down. She hated the carseat. She did not want to eat. She refused a pacifier. All the shushing and bouncing in the world did not calm her down. Since she was my second, I was exhausted by that time of day after taking care of a toddler and a newborn.

I thought I had made peace with my expectations of her sleep patterns and behavior. It took a few weeks to figure out she would probably spend most of her days attached to me and that she probably wouldn't sleep through the night at six weeks of age. Once I sat down in the car to go home and I burst into tears. I desperately wanted to rest and did not see 12 hour stretches of sleep or consistent, lengthy naps in the crib anywhere in my near future. You know how it is when you're sleep deprived and your entire world revolves around the needs of a newborn. Our expectations of what those newborn days look like are full of preconceived ideas based on who we know with kids, the photos we see, the movies we watch, the experiences we have with other babies.

Constantly comparing our experiences or expectations with other people's experiences and expectations robs us of our ability to embrace the moment we're in and love the kids, the job, the friends, the things we have. The pictures of perfection we expect or others expect us to have simply do not exist.

Every child is unique. This logical and perhaps unoriginal statement is probably the most difficult to walk out every day, because it means what works for one parent may not work for another. It also means we have to learn and pay close attention to the personality and needs of our own kids rather than trying to shape them into a frame of our own imposed expectations.

real life isn't picture perfect

A few of my friends are photographers and their experience behind the camera is more telling than the photos they take. We've all seen the quintessential newborn photo with the sleeping baby in a basket or on her tummy all curled up. The story behind the pictures is usually more interesting than the image itself.

One friend told me about how the baby squirmed around

constantly, pooped twice, and needed to be bounced back to sleep all within the hour long session. But you would never know based on the 5 gorgeous photos shared with family and friends.

There was a photo circulating a few years ago of a shirtless dad holding his naked newborn in a black and white photo. The baby has a small grin on his face and there is a stream of poo squirting out in a perfect arc. It's an amazing photo because it demonstrates the reality of newborn life, not the picturesque image most of us have based on advertising and the single perfect photo from the hundred that didn't turn out.

Why do we focus on getting the one perfect moment in an hour rather than embracing the whole hour itself (poo and all)? More often than not we rush around trying to stage a perfect moment even when cameras aren't around because of our own self-imposed expectations.

What if we embraced the reality of who we are and the kids we have instead of always trying to fit into a picture perfect image that never exists?

Real life is actually far more beautiful than the staged

moments. It's the beauty of a rose; one that is full of fragrant wafts of perfection paired with sharp and dangerous thorns always present to hurt. If we're attentive with the moments we have and handle with care, we can enjoy their beauty without feeling disenchanted or disillusioned when things don't look picture perfect. This awareness of thorns protects our hearts and minds from disappointment and frustration when things don't go according to plan.

Our best formed plans, hopes, expectations, and everything else that happens under the life umbrella rarely go the way we think they will.

The baby comes early or late. He is a c-section. We take the epidural instead of going all natural. We go all natural when we planned to have pain relief.

We want to nurse but for a hundred legitimate reasons can't do so and resort to bottle-feeding formula. We want to nurse and pump, but our baby refuses a bottle. We think she should eat every 3 hours, but she wants to eat every 2.5 hours.

Rather than sleeping all day like most newborns, our babies take 45 minute power naps. The baby sleeps all day and is up all night. Even if the sleep routine matches the book, we suddenly find our whole lives revolve around naps, and it feels like groundhog day over and over again.

We want to see them eating solids and crawling at a certain age. Heaven forbid they don't sit up on their own until a month after most other babies.

Our expectations about how and when things should happen should not dictate and frame our whole world, so that if they're not met all our peace and joy disappear.

memories of moments are framed by photos

Even before the birth of our kids, we have expectations surrounding the labor and delivery, their gender, and their personality.

The moments remembered most are the ones with photos. The photos themselves only tell part of the story and sometimes it's more about the picture itself and less about everything surrounding it.

My son Frederick's labor and delivery is a blur. The only reason I am able to remember it is through the photos my midwife took. We showed up at the hospital and an hour later he was born. Within that hour nurses and doctors rushed around me to figure it out and try to help keep his heartbeat from tanking during every contraction.

The cord was wrapped around his neck twice and every contraction sent his heartbeat plummeting. He was delivered via an emergency c-section and because it happened so quickly and I was pumped full of drugs, everything was and still is a fog.

I still can't remember the first time I held him or saw him. I have a picture of it which gives me a visual memory of the moment that I don't have an actual memory of. What I do know is I can clearly hear my husband announcing the news that we had a boy, which was shocking because we both secretly thought our baby would be a girl.

Throughout my whole pregnancy with Frederick, I planned for a natural delivery. I read all the books, talked with other moms. I mentally and emotionally prepared for a crisis free birth. There is no other moment in life that you can spend nine months preparing for while also having no control over. Memory and moments are funny. We remember things that happen through whatever lens of emotion or thoughts we had at that moment. Sometimes we reminisce and nostalgia takes over, causing us to think more fondly of a time than we normally would. Then there are moments that make you want to stop time altogether just to savor the beauty, peace, and joy of it.

Marcel Proust writes, "Remembrance of things past is not necessarily the remembrance of things as they were." Sometimes what we remember and how we remember it changes the way we think about the past and live in our present. By fully embracing the moment we're in, we stop reminiscing about the past and start looking forward to be wholly present without regret.

Every past experience we have informs the decisions we make regarding our future. Sometimes we look back at a photo and feel a rush of emotion from that moment. Before we have kids we don't hear about the stories of miscarriage, still birth, traumatic deliveries, and colicky babies. We don't realize that the photos we see tell a fraction of the story.

The picture of a mom holding her sleeping baby came after years of fertility treatment, tears, and heartbreak. The photo of a yawning infant came after the loss of older siblings and painful longing for a baby. Additionally, some moms have held babies whose photos were never shown because their life ended before it started. Some parents did not realize it would be the last photo of them with a newborn because of complications during delivery that makes having future children either too dangerous or just plain impossible.

We are immune to hearing these stories until our friends and family go through them and have the power to tell them. Our only frame of reference are the photos we see and the moments shared through social media. Even if we are aware of the potential or pain, loss, and complications, when it happens to us those moments are burned in our memories forever. They remain with us and part of us.

Some moments remain tattooed in our minds whether we have photographic evidence or not. Even when we expect the best and prepare for the worst, labor and delivery is the most unpredictable life event. You can't plan when it happens and you can't plan how it happens.

My daughter's birth day came, and the delivery was "textbook" according to my OB—no complications, no problems. The delivery was a perfect VBAC. But once she entered the world, she was completely unresponsive. The technical term is "cerebral decompression." For reasons still unknown, she did not breathe or have a heartbeat for 6 minutes. She was kept in the NICU for a week, and every nurse and doctor called her rapid recovery a miracle. Some moments like this one are engraved in our memories. The moment she was pulled off me by a team of 10 doctors who rushed in will remain with me forever, as well as the first time I saw her after she had been admitted to the NICU.

The photo of me seeing her alive in an incubator for the first time frames the way I remember the whole experience—tears of gratitude, pain, joy, and loss all in one moment. The raw emotion captured in that moment encapsulates the hours leading up to that moment as well as the days following as we waited for her to heal and come home.

the moments not pictured

When you become a parent some internal switch changes and you begin taking pictures of one subject *all the time*. Suddenly you realize you're phone storage is maxed and there are not enough hours in a day to weed through the thousands of photos you've taken of your one month old!

We've all seen the picture perfect moments of mom and baby cuddling and of dad with sleeping baby. The lighting is magical. The outfits, perfectly coordinated. I have a handful of selfies taken with Edith sleeping on me. They're sweet, precious moments of baby sleeping on mom, but there is more to the story than what you see in the photo.

Parenting, more often than not, happens in the moments before and after the photos: the crying (sometimes baby, sometimes mom), the pooping, the feeding, the bouncing, the rocking, the shhhsh-ing, the desperate longing for a shower.

When Edith was born, she spent the first week of her life in the NICU. She was not held 24/7 like most newborns during their first week of life. I don't know if this is the reason she screamed and cried nonstop unless being held the first 4 months of her life—and continued to adamantly fight to be held constantly into her toddler years. Or maybe it is simply her personality and when she wants what she wants, it's intensely apparent.

If I look closely at these perfectly captured selfies of her sleeping in my arms, I can see the exhaustion in my eyes. By the time she reached two weeks old, I quickly learned that she preferred to be held ALL the time. It's amazing how much you can love the moment you find yourself in as well as feel guilty about wanting or needing a break.

After two weeks, I began to take pictures of her falling asleep on me. Mostly because I wanted to document the post-fight moments. They were the moments when after 45 minutes of screaming and crying, she would finally fall asleep. The moments when I really wanted to put her down, but if I did she would wake up crying again and I would have to start all over. There are studies done that show stress is induced from hearing a baby cry. It's not pretty or healthy to hear a baby cry for long periods of time.

There is a photo of me wearing Edith in a wrap. It was a warm summer day, and I was sweating profusely while wearing her. She loved every minute of sleep snuggled up close. I think she was 4 weeks old in the photo, and I'd succumbed to her strength and need to be worn while sleeping during the day. Not pictured are the tears I shed just wanting a break to snuggle my two year old without having her strapped to me—mom guilt big time started to kick in! Guilt for desiring a break and guilt for not spending quality time with Frederick.

One of my favorite photos of her sleeping on me is on an airplane ride to Montana for my sister's wedding. Prior to the sleeping, Edie spent 30 full minutes screaming on an airplane because she was tired and fought sleep so much. I later found out, the couple sitting directly behind us were the photographers for my sister's wedding. At the wedding, I profusely apologized for being "those people" on the plane when I found out who they were. I strongly believe that life shouldn't stop when you have kids. We should not hop off the plane of life and become reclusive to avoid embarrassing or difficult moments. If we place our kids at the center of all our plans, our lives begin to rotate around their needs and wants like the earth around the sun. It's not healthy. Children are a blessing and we should never neglect their needs, but their wants should not dictate our days. We're the parents, and we get to frame the days and months and years of their childhood.

It's not easy to stay engaged socially with young kids, but for sanity's sake it's necessary to keep up on relationships with other adults. Sometimes the best way to remember the moment is to think about what was happening outside of what's pictured. The emotions, the thoughts, the activities both good and bad are part of the beautiful, short, sweet, and often painful seasons with babies and young kids.

One of my favorite verses of all time is Isaiah 40:11 (ESV)

where we see a picture of God as a shepherd holding and carrying lambs. It is a beautiful picture of what the first year of parenting is like—lots of close attention and bonding:

He will tend his flock like a shepherd;
  he will gather the lambs in his arms;
he will carry them in his bosom,
  and gently lead those that are with young.

When I first became a mom, God really began to speak to me through this verse about how He takes care of those who are young and helpless. He carries them close to His heart - it's such a beautiful picture of how loving He is towards us! What I love about this verse even more is the last part that says he will "gently lead those that are with young."

As a parent with babies and kids, it is easy to feel like the whole world is moving forward at a rapid pace and you're somehow frozen in time doing the same thing everyday at home. God has grace for every season of our lives and His grace for the season when we have young kids is a gentle leading. He doesn't drag us along or chastise us. He gently leads us, and where He leads us is close to Him so we can feel His heartbeat. It's comforting to know God watches out for those who watch over others.

make room for the unexpected

Once you become a parent, get a full-time job, begin school, or go through any other major life change, you have the choice to become more flexible with life or to find a routine and remain fixed and immovable based on your new schedule. I love schedules and routines and plans and predictable rhythms. I live for my calendar. It brings me indescribable joy to have a well-structured day. The only problem is the rest of the world will not bend to your baby's sleep schedule. This leaves you with two choices: become flexible and get out into society or become rigid and stay at home, bound to the clock.

One of the best pieces of advice my husband and I received as new parents had to do with flexibility. Someone told us after our firstborn was a few days old to let him sleep in the noisiest room for as long as possible. They encouraged us to hold him as often as we could those first few months, to bring him with us everywhere and incorporate him into our lives, to take a deep breath and embrace the extra time everything would take, to be flexible with his needs, and to be flexible with our own needs.

We brought him to two weddings before he was a month old. He joined our lives. We didn't stop living when he entered our family. Things definitely changed when he arrived, but we didn't cease living the way we had, we just altered how we did things and made room for the unexpected.

A few of my friends who don't have kids ask if life slows down when you have a baby. It does slow down. Some moments seem to last forever. Everything takes twice as long. It also speeds up. Months go by and you can't figure out where all the time went.

Whatever we did and wherever we went, I learned to prepare for the unexpected and to create buffer. We did say, "no" to some things, but for the most part we just continued to live life as before, but we made room around each activity knowing it would take longer and be less relaxing than we were used to.

I'm not saying this is the only way to parent. What I do find is your mindset determines the approach you take to parenting, work, marriage, friendship, and challenges in life. If you have a mindset of managed expectations, knowing full well things probably won't go as smoothly as you want, days will be full of interruptions and bumps in the road, life doesn't have to be put away on a shelf for the next 10 years while the kids are young. It means you expect things will be harder and take longer, but that's life and if you mentally prepare for it, you won't be frustrated or disappointed. Instead, you'll be able to laugh at the unexpected delays and unforeseen accidents that happen along the way. You'll be able to smile through all the interruptions because you've made room for them in your thinking and decided ahead of time that this is life in all its messy fullness.

Our kids are never the problem. Their needs shouldn't determine every minute of our day and equally we shouldn't force them to submit to our every demand. Our mindset and attitude determine the atmosphere of our homes and lives. When we make room for the unexpected, we don't react negatively to interruption.

2
capture the moment

Throughout every moment of every day we must decide what to fix our thoughts, attention, emotions, and willpower towards. In order to adjust our mindset to stay in a healthy place, we must become agile and flexible.

This requires effort and intentionality. It means we approach each challenge and each joy with a specific tool—either a telescope or a microscope. A lot of the little things we focus on don't matter at all and we need a bird's eye view and not a worm's eye view. On the other hand, a lot of the small moments need extra attention, examination, and appreciation because they are fleeting and ephemeral.

telescopic view

When you use a telescope, it's understood that there's a significant distance between you and your subject. When we choose to look with a telescopic view, we're creating distance between us and the current circumstance. It's a perspective we must have in difficult times because it allows us to focus on the big picture and gives us a longterm view when everything in us wants to wallow in momentary frustration, self-pity, doubt, insecurity, or any other emotion that rises up. It's something we must do during those first few days of our baby's life when complications with feeding arise and whatever frustrations or anxieties we're feeling overwhelm us. Taking a huge step back and out of the present time frame gives us freedom and peace to move forward without guilt or shame about our choices. The choices and decisions surrounding nursing and bottle feeding are fraught with emotion because of internal and external pressures. This is one of those moments where a telescopic view is so valuable and necessary.

I've talked with so many moms who feel guilt from a conflict between an internal desire to breastfeed and their inability or lack of joy when nursing. I've had countless conversations with women who find the societal pressure from family, friends, books, research is so strong externally that they're hardly able to see through their tears and pain.

We all want to live the best life possible. More often than

not, the best we have to offer comes from a place of peace and perspective. We give our best when we're not anxious, overwhelmed, and frustrated to the point of exhaustion. Follow the peace in your heart and zoom way out to see what this decision will look like 50 years from now.

There's no right or wrong way to do things. There is only a right or wrong way for you personally and that's what matters. Once we establish this within ourselves and move forward with grace for ourselves and for others who will make their own right decisions, we can love our kids, friends, and family from a place of security and confidence regardless of the external voices and criticisms.

We can often question and deliberate over the choices we make: the food we eat, the way we spend our time, and the things we prioritize. Every decision can make us anxious or it can teach us more about ourselves. They can cause us to search within for the best, life-giving option for every choice we make.

Talking with people you trust is a great way to gain a big perspective. If you're married, your spouse is the most important person and voice into your life. I can clearly remember the conversation my husband and I had about feeding our firstborn. We both agreed that if breastfeeding continued to be difficult and painful after 7 days, I would stop and we wouldn't look back or regret the decision. The timeline was arbitrary and personal, but it was something we agreed on and kept us at peace in the process of learning how to best take care of our son during that first week.

We must pull out our telescopes when our baby isn't sleeping through the night and every other baby we know is.

We must see the big picture when our toddlers refuse to eat their dinner, and it takes every ounce of energy to maintain self control.

We must gain a broad perspective when our babies takes short naps or cry all the way home in their carseats.

We must zoom out in time and think about how we want to remember the moment our preschoolers refuse to wear nothing but pajamas. How do we want our kids to remember those moments? How do we want to reflect on them in our golden years? Do we want our kids to remember us as constantly forcing our opinions and wills onto their choices? Do we want to remember our time as parents to young kids as days full of stress and frustration?

The days can be long and exhausting as a parent at home, an employee at work, a volunteer in an organization, and any other situation requiring endurance, but more often than not our perspective can alter our attitude, which shifts our outlook from cranky to hopeful.

Annie Dillard wrote one of the most powerful sentences that continues to speak to my soul. She said, "How we spend our days is, of course, how we live our lives." If we spend our days constantly annoyed, frustrated, and joyless, we should adjust our perspective because without realizing it, this can end up becoming the rest of our life. Choosing to focus on the big picture will bring peace, joy, and grace for yourself and your friends and family. Every day will continue to have its ups and downs, but our internal thermostat must intentionally choose to step outside the moment and see it from afar, to see it from another perspective in another time and season of life.

microscopic view

There are certain fleeting moments that deserve a pause, a reflection, a microscope. They are sweet and rare. They are the source of every hallmark card, poem, and nostalgic memory. It is these moments that remind us of the brevity of life. It's the time your baby first smiles, giggles, makes intentional eye contact. It's the look on her face when she's sleeping at the end of a long and tiring day, but you just can't stop looking at the long eyelashes and peaceful, relaxed face. It's watching an older brother put a protective arm around his younger sister and guide her around his friends or a new environment.

These are the moments we live for. They are the ones you want to bottle up and save for the days full of tantrums, outbursts, accidents, and surprises.

Heart bursting, gut wrenching joy marks these times when you get a glimpse into the purity of love you feel. No matter how many bad hours you've had, these are the moments that you must pull out your microscope.

Write them down. Take a photo. Examine every little detail with affection and attention. Remember the way the sun poured through the curtains and lit up the room while reading a book together. Remember the smell of freshly washed hair and clean pajamas. Remember the sound of uncontrollable laughter over silly jokes and pranks. Remember the way they skip the number four when counting to ten and how serious a game of hide-and-seek is.

Whether you're spending time with kids, close friends, or family, passionately observe and soak these moments in like a poet who takes in all the details and zooms in to collect all the information. The temptation to quickly move on is overwhelming, especially when there is so much to be done. If we continually rush through the time we're meant to savor, then we end up getting to the end of every day wondering how we survived rather than thrived. Throughout the day, pause, breathe deeply, and take in the whole scene and circumstance. Remind yourself to take moments and hold onto them for just a few seconds longer. These pauses will cultivate a habit of seeing and living life from a bigger perspective.

It's all about what, and how, and when we choose to devote our attention to. If we only pull the microscope out when times are tough and frustrating and remain in that frazzled state of disappointment or exhaustion, then that's all we'll remember from the time we have in the season we find ourselves in. The temptation to go on the downward emotional roller coaster and stay in a place of self-pity is overwhelming sometimes.

I remember the evenings when Edith was just a few weeks old and she would scream for three to four hours almost non-stop regardless of every attempt to calm her down.

These lengthy crying fits only lasted a week, but an hour into the crying on the third night I was heading down a dark emotional path, and there was a fork in the road: continue down the current path or take a different road marked by peace and joy.

It was a pre-determined and conscious choice to continue choosing the high road after another hour of crying, but I started singing the happiest songs I could think of. I started making songs up like, "this isn't going to last forever," and sang it while trying to calm my inconsolable baby down. I danced around the house and put on funny TV shows with subtitles so I could read the jokes over the crying. She wasn't an easy baby and this was the only method I found to cope with the intensity of her needs during those first three months.

She only slept well during the day if she was laying on me or being worn in a baby carrier. I remember wanting more than anything to just have an hour without having to hold her, so I could take a shower or do the dishes without this baby attached to me. But there came a day when I choose to embrace it. I decided that everything else could wait and being there to hold her while she napped was worth focusing on. Listening to her breathe, feeling to her heart beat, smelling her baby skin were all worth pulling a microscope out to pay attention to the details that quickly fade away.

Some parents love the newborn stage. Some parents love the toddler phase. Some parents love the elementary years. We are all naturally inclined towards a certain season of our kids' lives. Regardless of our natural leaning and personality preference, we all must find a place of peace and joy in every age and season. We should focus all our energy on being fully present for those moments when time seems to stop because what they're doing is so beautiful and perfect it makes you want to cry, or it's so silly and ridiculous you are crying tears of laughter. Begin the massive to-do list and throw on some happy music. Remind yourself that car trouble and repairs today are a blip on the screen of your life. Find something you find beautiful in the midst of the mess and focus on that one thing instead of the piles of laundry, bills, and dishes.

The poet Mary Oliver wrote, "attention is the beginning of devotion." The reason it's so important to give our attention to these ephemeral moments is because they are the origin of our affection. Our dedication to pay attention to the still small moments becomes a foundation for love, and if we can't stop and examine those moments every so often, we forget and miss out.

Since the day my son was born, he has been teaching me to slow down. He was a week overdue and that began what might just be his lifelong gift of teaching me to be patient and embrace the time I'm in. Because he seems to live and move at a different pace than almost any other person I know, I have learned to make space and room to just allow a moment to breathe. There have been so many times when we've been walking or eating or talking and I want so badly to move on to the next thing, but stop myself to wait for him.

On a walk to the park one day, he began to pick up almost every leaf that had fallen, examined it, and devoted all his attention to its beauty. I responded with the same "ooh" and "aah" as usual. By the time we arrived he had named his favorite leaf and was so connected to it that we couldn't leave it behind on our walk through the woods. I felt so challenged by his passion for a single leaf. There are things in life that are worthy of our focus that we miss out on because they are familiar or because we're busy pursuing our own interests.

perspective paradox

Every moment of every day we need to decide whether we're pulling out our telescope or microscope. A lot of the little things we focus on don't matter at all, and we need a bird's eye view instead of a worm's eye view. And a lot of the little moments need extra attention, examination, appreciation because they are so fleeting.

The perspective paradox is that we often pull out the wrong instrument for the current situation. We get caught up in the emotion of the difficult moments and find ourselves drowning when we should be soaring. We rush past the sweet stillness and miss a beautiful moment because we're too focused on what's coming up next.

Being a parent makes you so aware of time and timing. It's the paradox of knowing these days will someday be a wistful memory while also wishing the last few hours of the day away so you can put your feet up and breathe. It's attempting to live fully in the moment while also having eyes on yourself and recognizing this moment will be gone in the blink of an eye.

Even the Psalmist uses the contradictory nature of parenting to teach us something:

"For he gives to his beloved sleep.
Behold, children are a heritage from the Lord,

The fruit of the womb a reward."
Psalm 127:2-3 (ESV)

There are seasons when every mom and every dad pray for sleep. In this Psalm, the gift of sleep is followed by the gift of children which doesn't seem to make sense, especially if you have a colicky newborn or a toddler who wakes up early. This is the ultimate paradox. It's also the ultimate reminder that regardless of the amount of sleep we get, our kids are our greatest blessing and reward. Some of our greatest blessings are our biggest challenges. The dream job we've been hoping to get is exhausting and tireless. The relationship we longed to be in takes energy and effort we didn't realize. The house we buy consumes our time and money in ways we never imagined. Harvest in our lives always includes both blessing and work.

If you have ever talked with someone struggling with fertility, someone who desires a family but isn't seeing that desire fulfilled, you quickly realize how petty the complaints of a parent are. It's a reminder to have a grateful heart and to speak with humility about the kids, the job, the house, or the relationship we may have. You never know who is listening and there's always someone who doesn't have what you do.

I remember a conversation I had with someone who deeply longed to become pregnant and couldn't conceive even after medical support. She asked me about the birth of my four week son at a time when I was caught up in the pain and trauma of my recent c-section. I poured out my heart to her about the long recovery process and the difficulty with breastfeeding and the pain of sleep deprivation. In the kindest, gentlest way she said, "You're so blessed to have a healthy baby boy."

In that moment it felt like I was stabbed in the heart with a dagger. I almost burst into tears because I realized how incredibly selfish and oblivious my complaints were. Without any malice or resentment she spoke truth to my heart and it cut deep. From that encounter on, I was astutely aware that we do not know the pain, loss, or suffering some people experience. Our words and tone can either harm or heal the wounds some people carry due to miscarriage, infertility, stillbirth, illness, job loss, and a whole host of other heart breaking circumstances.

We are all aloof to the tender places in others' hearts, and it takes great strength to harness the words we say to people. Maybe you have the most amazing baby in the world who is beautiful, sleeps well, eats well, plays well, and while you have every right to brag about your gorgeous munchkin, it may be rubbing salt into an open wound of someone whose baby struggles with sleep, has health problems, or looks like an alien. Maybe the house projects that you are diving into with full fervor and energy that you can't stop talking about is painful for someone to hear about because they desperately long to move out of their apartment into a space of their own. Perhaps it's talking about the full-time work with great benefits and hours around people who have been job hunting for months or are working two part-time jobs to make ends meet. You never know who is listening and what they're going through.

There's a whole new level of self-awareness we grow into as parents. Having a baby and a toddler instantly puts a mirror up to your greatest flaws as they rise to the surface in ways you never expected. We find out what our lowest of lows looks like as well as what our highest of highs looks like, because our emotional range suddenly goes from extreme agony to ecstatic joy in ways we never thought possible.

The more we talk to our friends and family during the season we're in, the more we learn about their struggles and joys in the seasons they've been in and are currently in. These conversations hold great potential for growing in empathy and self-awareness.

I had the honor of interviewing my grandfather using the StoryCorps App. One of the questions I asked him was to share one of his most difficult experiences. He teared up as he told me about the baby who died one night in his sleep from sudden infant death syndrome. Over fifty years later, he still vividly remembered the pain of that loss. It isn't something he ever talked to me about before or after the interview, but I am grateful he felt safe enough to be vulnerable and share his pain with me that day.

I once heard two women who were a generation above me share the story of their stillborn babies. Their perspective on babies, toddlers, and kids came from such a place of peace and joy because they knew what it was to feel raw and broken from loss. As the told me their stories, I felt the weight of their loss as well as the wisdom of their encouragement to see my kids as a pure gift and treasure rather than a frustration or irritation.

Without stories like my grandfather's or stories from friends and family who experience loss in all the heartbreaking ways it can come, we can become calloused or ignorant to those around us and their journey. Our words and hearts have the potential to become a balm if we pause and reflect before vomiting every thought and emotion we have.

In parenting, as in life, our greatest challenge is to have a perspective that neither diminishes the beautiful nor exaggerates the ugly, that neither disregards the pain of others nor over-emphasizes the joy of our own experience.

faithful in the moment

"Let not steadfast love and faithfulness forsake you; bind them around your neck; write them on the tablet of your heart." (Proverbs 3:3, ESV)

faithful in your field

Throughout every season of our lives we have different fields to tend to, care for, and cultivate. In college it's usually your classes, community of friends and family, or maybe a part time job. After college there's a transition, it's your first job, community of friends and family, and maybe some volunteer commitments. Big transitions happen once you get married, settle in a city, buy a house, and maybe a baby comes along. Suddenly, the field narrows. Watching an infant can be equal parts daunting and boring. The whole world seems to move on while you're changing diapers, tending to late night feedings, and cleaning spit up.

I distinctly remember feeling as if the importance of what I was doing in life shrunk down to 2-3 hour chunks of time between feedings. It was humbling and challenging. One day when my son was a few months old, I cried tears of despair to my poor husband about how it felt like I was being left behind while everyone else was moving on with their big, important lives. Every field other than my own was much more appealing.

Regardless of the season we're in, field envy creeps in. Every lawn looks greener than our own, and discontentment festers. Rather than being faithful to the community and place we're in, we spend our energy focusing on the fruit and harvest in other people's lives while ignoring the goodness in our own backyard.

Ruth is a shining example of faithfulness in an unknown field. In this slim book, we see Ruth choose her foreign mother-in-law over the comfort of her own people. We see her move to a brand new region of the world, and embrace the lowly life of gleaning. There are a thousand opportunities for Ruth to become disillusioned with her new life and the season she was in. She probably felt like she had taken a step down on the social ladder—from wife and mistress in her own home to widow and gleaner in another's field.

Her integrity and diligence are inspiring and also challenging. She woke up every day to collect scraps left behind the paid harvesters. Her station was lowly and humble. At any point in time she could have called it quits, but she persisted joyfully and patiently. Had she given up, she would have never met her future husband, had children, and redeemed her story. She ends up marrying Boaz, a wealthy and respected landowner. She becomes the great-grandmother to David, king of Israel, and is recorded in the lineage of Jesus.

We should never diminish or underestimate the implications of our actions. When we fully embrace the field we find ourselves in and faithfully look after its contents, we discover a harvest waiting for us that is bigger and better than anything we ever imagined. Whether you work full-time, part-time, go to school, or stay home with kids, be wholly present and fully faithful in the field you find yourself in. The fruit of your labor far exceeds the missed opportunity brought on by lamentation. Whatever field we're in, we must work. It's tiring. It's trying. It's repetitive. It feels never-ending. The work of sowing seeds, tending plants, and cultivating growth is unseen and unglamorous.

My first vegetable garden looked unimpressive and pitiful in its beginning days. The carrot and beet seeds didn't sprout for a month, the lettuce and kale seeds emerged after a few weeks, and the starter tomato and pepper plants looked like a strong breeze would uproot them. Every day for the first month I watered, weeded, and tended a small dirt patch. It felt like nothing would come from this minuscule field. Then one week, everything emerged and exploded. Every week after that the plants grew, almost to the point of being unmanageable. Once the harvest started, we didn't know what to do with all the produce.

We can often find ourselves belittling the small, insignificant details that make up our days as we walk around our current field. Whatever we value and care for in a season that feels small and in a field that looks bare will yield an abundant harvest. This is the difficulty of faithfulness. It's unseen, unknown, and unappreciated in the moment. But if we can begin to value and elevate the simple, everyday tasks, then the vision and expectation of our field increases. It's about taking care to do simple things full of love and passion. I came to a place where I had to ask myself about the things I actually cared about in life. What type of mom did I want to be? What type of wife? Friend? Sister? Daughter? The characteristics I wrote down for each of these began to inform the way I approached everyday tasks.

I wanted to be a mom who was present, thoughtful, and patient. I desired to nourish my kids with healthy food and provide an environment that cultivates creativity and curiosity. These desires shaped the minutes of my days. I no longer felt guilty for focusing on making food while my son played or whined or demanded my attention. It was important that he saw me use fresh food and do the best I could to create balanced meals. I discovered that a safe and uncluttered space left babies and toddlers with room to discover and explore on their own. I stopped feeling guilty for not buying all the new toys and having an abundance of stuff to prevent boredom. Boredom is healthy. It's necessary for internal creativity. When I was able to verbalize the values that I held dear to my heart, it freed me to stop comparing my field to someone else's. It allowed me to stop judging other people's values, and it created a contentment and healthy pride in the small field I called my own in the season I was in.

peace in the process

Parenting is a long distance marathon that requires faithfulness and perseverance every day. It's a lifelong journey that begins the day you conceive.

Cultivating peace in the process produces rest for the journey.

It's essential to make a decision in advance that peace will guard your heart and mind regardless of the situation so that when faithfulness is required it rises up. We need the faithfulness to continue doing the right thing even when times get tough and the perseverance to continue moving forward full of faith even when things look grim.

When I found out I was pregnant with my first child, I read about natural birth and breastfeeding in books for pregnant women. Towards the end of my second trimester, I picked up books about babies and their first year of sleeping, eating, and playing. At every check-up, my midwife would ask me about my birth plan and I told her it was the only thing in my entire life I had no control over. There was no control over the date, the length, the pain, or the process. She asked whether I planned on taking drugs for pain. I told her it depended on how I felt in the moment and that I wanted to do my best to go without, but I wasn't against using them. She asked whether I wanted to nurse or bottle feed and I shared that while I really wanted to breastfeed, I saw several friends struggle to the point that it hindered the first few months of bonding and produced more stress than peace. She asked how I felt about every other detail related to the birthing process and I continued to respond that I wouldn't know until I reached those moments.

By nature, I am a planner. I like schedules and routine and structure. When pregnant, I decided way ahead of time to not plan anything too specific when it came to labor, delivery, and the first few months, because it was entirely unpredictable and out of my control. I prayed everyday for a healthy baby who would be peaceful and joyful. My son was one week overdue and that last week was agonizing. I just wanted to meet my baby. I went into labor while in a movie theater with my sister and spent the whole night counting contractions and the time between them. In the morning my husband took me to my already planned midwife appointment who after monitoring me and checking my progress promptly sent us to the hospital.

I had progressed enough to be admitted. The baby's heart rate dropped with every contraction and needed to be watched closely. Within one hour of being admitted, I was rushed in for an emergency c-section because the heartbeat plummeted further down each time. While I didn't want to have surgery, I felt peace throughout the mad rush to the operating room.

I was terrified and at peace in the same breath.

The cord was wrapped around my son's neck twice and could have killed him. He is alive and well today because of the expertise of the doctors, nurses, and midwife who were present. Labor and delivery is a small part of my parenting journey and a smaller part of my life journey, but it's a pivotal one. Women forever remember the stories of their births because it's the opening chapter of their children's lives.

This birth experience shaped my faith in God and showed me how faithful he is. When I started to talk to my doctor about birth plans for my second child, I was afraid to hope for a natural delivery. She encouraged it and suggested we try, but if complications arose she would want to do surgery.

Throughout the whole pregnancy, I prayed for a peaceful labor and delivery that didn't result in surgery. My husband and I decided ahead of time that even if our hopes for a natural birth weren't met, we would be at peace in that process. My daughter arrived on her due date and announced her intention to enter the world with my water breaking. My contractions were immediately intense and 8 hours later she was born. The labor and delivery were textbook according to my doctor. Everything happened the way it was supposed to. There were no red flags, no big or small concerns. It was perfect.

They placed her on my chest and within 30 seconds she was pulled off me because she showed no signs of life. An emergency team rushed in and began chest compressions and all other forms of intervention to save her life. For six whole minutes she was non-responsive. They called it a cerebral decompression in her medical records. She spent six days in the NICU recovering and growing strong enough to come home.

It was a short stay because her recovery was, according the doctors, miraculous. It was a miracle. She was a miracle.

This event was traumatic for her as much as it was for me. The six minutes felt like hours. The six days felt like years. Throughout it all, Isaiah 33:6 (ESV) rang through my heart,

"And he will be the stability of your times."

God will be the peace, the rest, the strength, the security, the safety, the dependability, and the health of your times. Regardless of the emotional ups and downs—and they were many—he was present. And although I felt the intensity of it all, I also knew the peace of God through it all.

The process of her being in the NICU required a faith and trust that I never needed before. It pushed me closer to God and he began to show me that if I could have peace in this process now, I could have peace in every process to come for the journey ahead as a mom of two kids.

One of the things Jesus' sacrifice bought for us is permanent rest. Part of our inheritance as Christians is the ability to live from a place of rest instead of continually striving to attain it.

If you're a parent, you begin this epic odyssey the day your baby entered the world. Every step along the way requires peace because it's a process. Sleeping in consistent ways is a process. Eating food as a baby, toddler, and school aged kid is a process. Potty training is a process. Learning to be kind and empathetic is a process. Schooling is a process. Letting them make mistakes is a process. Each and every stage in the journey can be marked by peace, but we must make a predetermined decision to let peace reign. It's the same when you begin dating someone and you feel it moving towards marriage. It takes peace to trust the timing of God to bring you and your future spouse together. Peace is necessary when you decide to put roots down and buy a house or maybe not put roots down and travel for a season. The same goes for finding a job and the sometimes lengthy and painful process of applying, interviewing, and landing a position somewhere.

This does not mean every moment feels peaceful. It means that the state of our hearts continually returns to a calibrated peace that comes from the Holy Spirit. It means that the Prince of Peace is present every step along the way guiding us and ministering to us when we need it most. He is faithful every moment of every day. And even when we want to give up and throw in the towel, his faithfulness brings us back, stirs our faith, and gives us perseverance to keep pursuing Jesus in every situation.

miracle in the mundane

For 27 years I lived a productive, fast-paced, long hours, deeds-centered life. I lived for my to-do lists in school and work. After two and a half years of juggling school and a career with kids, I became a stay at home mom. No matter what season you're in, living in the understanding that what you do is not who you are is challenging. Our identity does not come from the things we do; it comes from who God has made us to be.

I am a mom. My husband is a dad. These roles are important, vital, necessary, and an absolute privilege, but they are not who we are fully. There are days when it feels like it. There are days when the laundry is piled high, the dishes are growing crusty, the toilets are dingy, the floors are mucky, the kids are finally asleep, and all we have the energy to do at the end of the day is crash, hoping tomorrow is better.

No matter what we spend most of our hours doing, there will be boring and mundane tasks that require regular attention. The greatest challenge is living full of wonder and expectation to see beauty in everything. Seeking, finding, and making miracle in the mundane is a constant process.

Lingering long enough to savor the mystery of the gift of life that's all around us can feel like an inner battle. I remember clearly the day this dawned on me. My son was a very alert newborn who required little sleep to eat and play happily. He loved to engage with his environment as fully as possible even at a few months old. I was frustrated one fall day that I couldn't leave him to quietly coo by himself in a bouncy chair or contentedly lay down on a blanket with toys, so I put him in the stroller and went for a walk around the neighborhood. The leaves were brilliant oranges, reds, and yellows. The sky was vivid blue. The air was crisp and smelled like earth and dying leaves. Every step echoed loud crunches. Halfway through our walk it dawned on me that this day, this moment was miraculous. The change of seasons is an extraordinary event to witness and I dismissed it because my focus was elsewhere.

There is no such thing as an identical leaf. It took my son to pull me out of my inner world of frustration to see the absolutely stunning miracle taking place just outside the four walls of my home.

Walking along, I realized that there is constantly miracle in the mundane, and all we need to do is discover it.

There are still moments, and many of them, when this isn't in the front of mind. But this conviction resounds in my heart and has become a mantra in my thoughts. It's the way a rain drop trickles down the window. It's the silence of snow falling. It's the early morning sunlight that sneaks through the curtains. It's watching water pour out of a faucet whenever I need it. It's the way a baby holds onto your finger so tightly. It's sticking clothes in a machine, adding soap, turning it on, and pulling them out clean. These everyday activities are astonishing. We must never overlook the details that make up our lives because there's beauty to behold if we choose to perceive it and then pause to notice it.

Sometimes the miracle is something we can do for someone else—we can be an answer to someone's prayer when we choose to step outside ourselves and into a world ripe with opportunities to display the love of God. It's as simple as sending an encouraging message to someone who randomly popped into your head. It could be striking up a conversation with someone at the library or the store. Maybe it's giving someone money who needs it. Perhaps it's praying with someone in need of support or breakthrough.

Whatever little gesture rises in your heart, do it. The more we step out and meet someone else's need, the more beauty and miracle we see in the world.

maximize the moment

"The wisest of women builds her house, but folly with her own hands tears it down." (Proverbs 14:1, ESV)

Leaders in our sphere

Whether we want to admit it or not, we dictate the atmosphere and climate of our environments. For a brief period of time, we have great influence in our children's lives and what we do with that matters a lot. Between the ages of zero and five (some research says even up to eight) years old, most of a child's core development occurs and their belief systems are established. This is a daunting thought. Wherever we find ourselves in life, we have a short window of time to make an impact on the lives of those around us—in our workplace, school, and home.

The amount we are able to exhibit self-control and lead by example is of utmost importance. Our foundation must be solid and strong in God in order to bring hope, love, joy, peace, and order to the environments we find ourselves in. We are the leaders of our homes, jobs, and classrooms. This has been a massive revelation in my life because it means I must take initiative to do something first. Rather than continually submitting to the whims and wishes of whatever mood we're in or whatever mood our kids or the people around us are in, we take charge and decide to forge a new path marked by confidence in our roles in the season and place we find ourselves in.

I can remember when I was pregnant with my second and my first was just over a year old. We had a puppy at the time who was full of energy and life. I realized one day that the attitude I conveyed toward our dog, Winston, would be the same attitude my son would have. One morning, I came into the living room after changing Frederick's diaper to discover Winston chewing our leather couch. I was furious because I had just finished feeding and walking him. What else could I do for him? This dog had peed on every square inch of hardwood floor, he had bitten through countless leashes, and required constant attention to keep him out of trouble. Deep down inside I was boiling and it was about to overflow, but with one look at Frederick I realized that even at a young age he would absorb my reaction and it would impact his outlook on Winston. So I took a deep breath and very sternly commanded Winston to stop chewing the couch and promptly moved him out of the living room.

These moments happen a thousand times every day. The trash can gets knocked over, the freshly cleaned laundry is dragged through dirt, the water bottle spills, the newly scrubbed toilet has pee sprayed all over it, the white blanket has chocolate smeared on it. Our response to these momentary problems affects the way our kids react to and respond to crisis in their own lives. When we reduce the intensity of the moment with a calm, calculated version of "oh no" rather than a freak out, we're leading by example. When we're able to shrug off something that really frustrates us with a "we'll do better next time" attitude rather than an end of the world meltdown, we're leading by example. When we laugh at the ridiculous nature of the moment instead of being swallowed up by the emotion we feel, we're leading by example. While it is so important and essential for others to see us be vulnerable and emotional, we should lead by example and with self-control when it comes expressing those emotions. We can be constructive in our expression of anger, frustration, disappointment, sadness, and any other mood under the sun.

One morning, both my kids decided to create a mural on a wall in our house. It was an epic masterpiece in their minds. My husband and I got an extra 15 minutes of sleep because they were finally playing together nicely. When I first discovered the deep purple and pink sketches all over the wall everything in me was screaming, "why can't anything stay nice for just one day!" I think I had just cleaned up marker from the carpet the day before and was still reeling from that experience. If I was to build my house in this moment rather than tear it down, my reaction mattered a lot. I was very stern and expressed how upset I was in the calmest way possible. It took massive amounts of self control to say, "What did you guys do? This is not where we color with markers. We are going to wash this wall and paint over it." Inside I was dying to myself a thousand times over. I just wanted to sleep in past 7 a.m. and not have to worry about the house being torn apart. I desperately wanted the picture perfect room from photos. These desires weren't wrong, they were just misplaced in the line of priorities.

Priority number one:
provide a loving and secure environment for growth

Priority number two:
create healthy boundaries that allowed for freedom and safety

Priority number three:
create a space that our whole family felt at home

If I wanted these priorities to take precedence, I had to surrender the desire for the neat, tidy, clean, and perfect. My life was beautiful. My kids were healthy. I had food in the cupboards. We had more than enough clothes and toys. While I still greatly value order and beauty in the home, these must fall into line after my other priorities and not preempt them. I want my kids to see that we take care of and value our environment, but not to the point where they're fearful to make mistakes, explore, and bravely try new things.

Wherever you are in life, you must settle in your own heart and mind what your priorities will be for yourself in the place you're in. Take some time to think about what these will be, write them down, and be confident in your choices. Once you have landed on them, let everything else that isn't a priority fall away or into line. Focus on ways to bring those things in your heart out and foster an environment that will allow those things to flourish.

upward and downward growth

There are a certain metaphors for getting older and maturing that we often use. We speak about our maturity in the architectural sense as building, and internal growth by referencing nature. While kids explore and develop and get older, we always have the opportunity to continue maturing and growing. Before kids come along, we have no idea how much we don't know. Suddenly they show up and it's as if a giant spotlight turns on highlighting our strengths, weaknesses, perfections, and flaws.

We must grow upward in stature like a building to support our families as well as downward in inner strength like a tree to stand strong in every season. If you're a parent, so much growth happens as a direct result of the growth and maturity of your kids. They can be the greatest stimulus and cause of maturity if we allow our hearts to be soft and malleable. Growth happens whenever we allow ourselves to be molded and shaped to be more Christ-like through the experiences and environments that we're in when we choose patience over frustration, love over offense, grace over justice.

When my daughter was just starting to speak in full sentences, she started saying, "oh my gosh!" all the time.

At first, I was completely baffled. A day or so later, I heard myself saying "OH MY GOSH!" in a frustrated tone as I wrestled both kids into the car. I had a complete out of body moment where I realized everything I said was heard by both my kids. All day, every moment of every day, I had little sponges following me around soaking up my words, tones, attitudes, gestures, opinions, beliefs. Talk about intimidating! You may have had a similar experience if you manage people in a team or in the workplace. What we say resonates more than we realize.

We all have those moments in time when we realize what we do is being so closely observed and watched that it makes you want to crawl under a rock and never come out again. There is no way I could remain the wide-eyed, deer-in-the-headlights mom I once was. This was especially true as my kids reached school age. I needed to build new habits and attitudes to support new experiences. I had to dig deep into my relationship with God in order to become so rooted and inwardly strong that the circumstances and storms of life would not cause me to crumble.

upward growth

We must all find the rhythms, rituals, and habits that work

best for each of us in order to build upwards to support growth. The difficulty comes when you compare what works for others with what works for you and your own needs. Depending on your own personality, lifestyle, work, family, and friend commitments, you will have to discover through trial and error what works best for you and your tribe.

Some things are as simple as choosing to use disposable or cloth diapers. There are strong opinions on either side of what should be a simple decision. I had to have an honest assessment of my life in order to decide what would work best for our family. Something as small as this can throw anyone into a mini-bout of turmoil. You must listen to the rhythm of your life and be authentic to who you are to discover the habits and rituals that work for you.

The beautiful thing about having a rhythm is that it's flexible and agile. It can change depending on the season. The tempo can increase or decrease, but we must learn to be sensitive to those subtle shifts in order to adjust.

When it was just my husband, me, and my son, I worked part-time and this schedule provided a rhythm that brought peace and joy to our home. I spent my mornings working while he played with his friends at a daycare down the street, and I spent the afternoon getting things done and relaxing while he napped. When he woke from his nap, we played and then I would make dinner. It was a sustainable tempo for our lives until my daughter was born. While I continued to work the first six months of her life, it was not a pace I could maintain. What was once beautiful in its season became hectic, chaotic, and there was little time for me to actually connect in a meaningful way with either of my kids.

Quitting my part-time job meant a big change in our daily rhythms. It was tempting to stay in my PJs all day long and for the first few weeks, I did. After a few weeks hanging around the house without any structure or rituals to our days besides nap time, I realized I needed to figure out what habits I wanted to have in our lives during this season. What things did I value? What brought joy to my life? What purpose grounded me between changing diapers and feeding hungry babes?

These were questions I began to ask myself. It was a stretching transition. As I began to answer these questions for myself, without comparing my answers to what I saw other people doing, things came into focus and I discovered the rhythms that worked for me.

Each day was unique in content, but it had an underlying framework that worked until both kids were walking and talking and I began working part-time again. Until I became a parent, I didn't realize how quickly I would need to adapt and change. It's so swift and constant, I often find myself struggling to readjust. Every three to six months, it feels like a new wind blows and while the daily rituals and values remain the same, the components of each day alter slightly to the rhythm of the moment.

For two whole years I read, tracked, and studied the Bible on my phone because it was convenient and necessary to keep pace with two tiny ones needing constant attention. Then one day I realized I loved papers and pens and all things tangible, and I finally had the time and energy to go back to these things I found so much joy in. It was a small, yet subtle change that made a big difference to my habits. Rather than having my face buried in my phone, I began to use it less frequently and worked with pen and paper while my kids colored and crafted. It was a new, fresh rhythm that made me feel like me again.

What works in one season may not work in the next. This is the constant challenge with all things in life. Change is constant. As our seasons in life change, we must continue to grow and learn as well. Our greatest difficulties arise when we continue trying old methods from yesterday rather than seeking fresh wisdom for today.

downward growth

The depth of the foundation directly affects the height of a building. Living in Toronto during my undergrad, I remember watching in awe as skyscrapers went through all their phases of development. Something that surprised me was the amount of time that went into digging a crater-sized hole before any actual construction work began. The foundation of each new skyrise was massively deep. We had friends visiting one weekend, and one of them was familiar with architecture. He began describing in great detail the amount of effort and calculation that went into building these new condos and buildings. I learned from him that the strength of each building was directly connected to how far down the foundation went.

For the first five years of your kid's life you have an amazing window of time to put deep, strong foundations in their hearts and minds. This is daunting and sometimes overwhelming. When our own foundations go deep into God and we continue to extend our roots into his love, we are far more capable of raising kids with a healthy perspective on themselves and the world around them. Healthy boundaries and a continual demonstration of unconditional love are without question an amazing foundation for any child. The thing is boundaries that work for one may not work for another.

When my daughter was close to one year old, she was ready to move to a bigger car seat. We were given a used one from some friends but the buckle on it was difficult to get open. For the first few months, I struggled to to use it and each time I went to get her out it took far longer than it should. One cold and snowy winter day, I was shivering as I tried to wiggle the buckle open. God spoke to me through the struggle. He showed me that in order to unlock what was in her I had to learn the best method. With careful attention, I would begin to grow in my understanding of her and the life God wants her to lead.

A few months later, the lock on her door would get stuck every so often and I would have to climb over the front seat to pull it up to open the door. God is so kind to remind us of things he speaks. I was instantly convicted that I had not been seeking him for the unique keys needed to help her mature. After that day, I began to pray and ask God for specific wisdom for each of my kids to help their foundations go deep.

In one single moment of time, my perspective and outlook changed from one of frustration and tiredness to one of hope. If we're not careful, we can forget these small moments because we're rushing on to the next thing. I missed the revelation the first time God spoke to me because I didn't slow down to fully listen. I heard but didn't listen. Something I know to be true for myself is that I feel the constant pull to keep moving on to the next thing. The art of slow does not come naturally, especially with phones and social media and the constant need to feel connected to something other than the moment I'm currently in.

In the first chapter of the book of Psalms, it describes the person who trusts in God as a tree whose roots go deep and whose leaves flourish. Our roots as believers should continue to deepen throughout every situation and circumstance that tests our faith, patience, or hope. The trust we have in God and his character and his nature will directly affect the depth of our relationship with him.

We lead by example wherever we are, and when our foundation is secure, it directly affects the lives of those around us. They see us go through difficulties, and they learn from our reactions and moods more than all the lecturing in the world. They watch our every move, and they are true copycats.

When we're able to work through something challenging and our kids and those around us witness that on a consistent basis, they mimic our resilience in the face of difficulty. The greatest gift we can give is a foundation of trust in God regardless of what's happening. When our lives continue to produce fruit even in trying seasons, our kids experience firsthand the results of being deeply rooted in God.

Take a few moments to reflect on the times you've heard God speak to you about your kids or anyone you are responsible for. Find a place to write those keys down and begin to slow down to listen to his voice in those still small moments of time that so quickly pass us by. He always desires that we grow closer to him just as we desire to grow closer to them.

5

rest in the moment

"Even the sparrow finds a home,
  and the swallow a nest for herself,
  where she may lay her young,
  at your altars, O Lord of hosts,
  my King and my God." (Psalm 84:3 ESV)

a nest for herself

These verses from Psalm 84 speak about the care and thought concerning even small creatures like mother birds. The fact that God cares about the sparrow and the swallow enough for them to find a home, a nest, and a safe place to keep their young in his presence is amazing. He cares about even the smallest and lowliest of animals. His eye does not miss a single detail of our days.

He makes sure there is a space for the sparrow and swallow

to worship and be at home even though they have squawky, needy babies vying for their attention and needing their care. This passage is especially powerful for parents of young kids who struggle to remain engaged spiritually or socially after starting a family. God has a special place in his presence carved out for those with young ones. This season of life is meant to be lived near to him—constantly coming to the altar as a living sacrifice. God desires for these insignificant birds to create a home for their young, a safe nest where the babies encounter the presence of God and they grow up knowing the sound of worship.

This picture demonstrates the tenderhearted, kind love of our Father as we embark on the journey of caring for others, whether it's in the home, the workplace, or the church. There are a few things about the nest that stand out. First, it's a place of comfort for everyone abiding in it. Second, it's a place that continually remains in the presence of God. And lastly, it's in a space that ministers to both the parents and the babies. These aspects speak to embracing a lifestyle of rest amidst a flurry of daily activities. In order to rest in the moment, we must create space in our lives for sanity time, discovering beauty in the now, and keeping our tanks full.

sanity time

Shortly after the birth of my second child, I was running on empty. Not a single drop of energy remained at the end of the day. She refused the bottle, refused to sleep unless held or carried, and didn't settle for the night until 10 or 11. I woke with both her and my firstborn around 6 am and spent the whole day meeting both their needs. Thankfully, my second still took an afternoon nap so the load lightened for an hour or two everyday. But Edith needed to sleep on me or else she would wake and cry inconsolably until calmed down again. So I spent the first two months sleeping in the afternoon with her on me when I could. What my husband found after two months of long days with little to no breaks for "me time" was a burnt out woman in desperate need of rejuvenation.

He implemented a Sanity Night once a week where I left the house for 2-3 hours and did what refreshed me. Every single person needs time out to do something that brings joy and refreshment to the soul. In order to be at your best, you must have the opportunity to replenish your supply and that means taking care of yourself. Our culture encourages independence, self-sufficiency, and having it all. While not all new parents may find this season difficult, many do because the sublime message we hear throughout our lives is a DIY, figure-it-out-yourself mantra. And when we do reach out for help, be it from the internet or other seasoned parents, we are inundated with personal opinion and bias with specific details that may or may not be helpful for our own unique problems.

One of the best things we can do for ourselves is receive practical help when it's offered and ask for help when it's needed. Different personalities will react differently in times of need, but God never intended for us to remain in isolation while raising young kids. He desired for us to live in a space close to him and close to the people in our lives who are safe and encouraging. While we are encouraged to offer our lives up as living sacrifices, we are never called to martyr ourselves and our own needs as we care for others. God has given us the unique and extraordinary privilege of taking care of his kids. If we neglect our own needs and desires completely, we will end up resenting this amazing gift and this will produce a ripple effect in the people we care for in other important relationships.

Ask for help when you need it. Accept help when it's offered. Carve out time during your week where you can do the things that make you feel fulfilled and revitalized. By maintaining your own sanity, you will have energy and the ability to care for the young in your nest.

beauty in the now

Sometimes we need to rest in the glorious mess that parenting produces. We need to plop down and just laugh at the moment we find ourselves in. Cultivating an eye to see *beauty in the now* can be challenging, but not impossible. Our homes should be a place where we create an atmosphere of comfort and the type of rest that comes from knowing God and going to him every moment of every day with our cares, concerns, worries, and anxieties.

When we release the things in our hearts that frustrate or worry us and give them to God, we create a nest that fosters rest in the presence of God. Seeing *beauty in the now* means we play music that lifts our spirits and souls. It means we keep our hearts clean and pure, not holding onto offense and bitterness. It means we take stock of the things in our lives that produce joy and focus on them while removing the things that weigh us down or add stress.

Savoring the things that bring beauty to your life is essential to loving this season. It can be as small as taking a moment to gaze at a ray of sunlight pouring through a window, even if your inbox is full or toddler is whining. It can be as big as going through your home and getting rid of clutter to free your space of unneeded items that accumulate over time. Sometimes a good spring clean of your environment causes you to see the beauty in the now because it's fresh and new again. Sometimes spending a few dollars on some flowers to add some color to the room you spend the most time in is worth all the gold in the world.

Whatever you need to do to discover *beauty in the now* is worth it. The nest you have should reflect the beauty of God's presence. It doesn't need to be perfect or even close to perfect, but it should bring you joy because you are able to produce and see something beautiful everyday.

keeping your tank full

If you are a parent of young kids, it's important to remember that God's presence can inhabit your home. We have access to everything we need to live our lives, but in the midst of our sleep deprived and stressed out states we must go to the source of all life. We must see that as Christians we have streams of living water in us and we can tap into its flow to remain full.

Our mental tank takes a beating during stretches without sleep. The brain doesn't work well on too little sleep. When we're at our weakest, we must go to God and people who can encourage and strengthen us. Sometimes we don't realize how much we're affected by lack of sleep until someone shines a light on our lagging mental capacity. In order to keep your mental tank full, a nap and time to do nothing is the best medicine. The difficulty is spotting the opportunity. If you have a child who isn't sleeping through the night and they take a nap during the day, give yourself permission to sleep when they sleep. It sounds incredibly boring and ridiculously simple, but it will fill your tank with much needed mental and physical energy. Similarly, if your job requires you to work in the evening or on weekends, don't feel bad about taking time out during other parts of the week to rest.

Our emotional energies wear thin after continually meeting the needs of the young in our nest. This applies to any type of management or leadership, but it's especially true for parents. This loss of energy becomes especially clear as the end of the day draws near. The closer it gets to dinner and bedtime, the less patience and resilience we have to maintain a positive outlook and attitude. That's why it's important for you figure out what replenishes your emotional energy and begin to use it to keep yourself full.

I realized one day that the time I spent preparing dinner was the worst hour of my day. We were all tired and ready for a change in scenery. One afternoon, I steeled myself for the onslaught of whining, complaining, and getting into trouble while I cooked by playing dance music. It instantly changed the whole atmosphere in my heart. It lifted my emotions from a 2 to a 10. When one kid got hurt and the other did something mischievous, I had the emotional energy to react well. As the complaints piled up, I responded with lyrics from the song or a spin around the room. It sounds silly, but it made a massive difference. It's one key of many that can prevent our emotional tanks from running on empty.

When we have little energy to do anything in the little downtime we have, our natural inclination is to replenish every area of our lives before replenishing our spirits. But the source of all life comes from our intimacy and connectedness to God. If we keep this connection strong and growing, it will spill out and affect every other area. Figuring out ways to keep your spiritual life vibrant is essential to thriving in this season. Like the sparrow and swallow, we must make our home in the presence of God and dwell there. It isn't a place we visit from time to time, it's a place where we abide. This doesn't mean we spend every second of every day doing super spiritual things, but it does mean we keep an ongoing dialogue with God. We converse with him because he leans in to hear what we have to say. We stop and listen to hear what he has to say.

Something I found immensely helpful to maintaining a full spiritual tank was reading one Psalm every day. I would write down just one line (sometimes on my phone, sometimes in a notebook) that really spoke to me and throughout the day would come back to it again and again. This single verse sustained my spiritual life everyday. And everyday there was something fresh to restore my spirit. Jesus, the Word of God, tells us to come to him and when we do, we'll receive the bread of life. This living bread is something we must take a hold of. It's always available, but we must take it for ourselves and feed on it expecting nourishment and provision.

When we spend time filling ourselves up on good food rather than filling ourselves with mindless scrolling through social media, we'll have all we need to give to those around us who need our care, attention, and love. Maintaining a flourishing inner life will cause us to overflow, and it will directly affect every other area of life. The outer circumstances may differ each day, but when your soul and spirit are taken care of, you'll respond with more grace, peace, patience, and joy regardless of the difficulty.

6
power of the moment

"All your children shall be taught by the Lord, and great shall be the peace of your children." (Isaiah 54:13 ESV)

Most people's beliefs about themselves, the world around them, and other people are almost completely solidified between ages five and eight. This is a daunting realization. Whether you believe more strongly in nature or nurture, this formation at a young age happens. As parents we have a window of opportunity to influence our kids in the best way possible before they are deep in the school age years. In work and church life, we have a similar window of opportunity with younger co-workers and new believers.

We get to speak into the lives of those younger than us and demonstrate positive examples of problem solving, self-esteem, empathy, forgiveness, security, affection, generosity, and healthy lifestyles. This list is never-ending because our actions speak louder than our words, and kids especially are sponges who soak everything up. I can say all the right things about trying to solve a difficult problem when my son is attempting to figure something out. But if I immediately give up every time I'm faced with a difficult situation and speak about the impossibility of circumstances the words I speak mean nothing.

I'm not a naturally handy, crafty person. One day I wanted to figure out how to set up the double stroller we bought in preparation for baby number two. I ordered the extra pieces needed to set it up, and the day they came in the mail I went to work. Frederick was a year and a half old and shadowed me all day long. After 30 minutes of unsuccessful attempts, I was sweating and on the verge of giving up. Throughout the entire process I carried on a dialogue with my son that consisted of phrases like, "Oh, I think this will work!" and "This might be it!" and "We've got this!" After lots of trial and error, I finally figured it out and asked Frederick for high five and thanked him for being my helper.

Having kids means you suddenly have an extra pair of eyes on yourself and they see you at your best and worst. This is a good thing. If we are at our worst and are able to demonstrate how to pull ourselves out of a really bad situation or emotion, our kids will learn that everyone has bad days but those days don't determine who we are or what our outlook on life will be.

One time my husband and I were having somewhat of a heated disagreement and our three year old looked at us both and said in all seriousness, "You guys need to be nicer to each other and forgive each other." In those moments of extreme emotion where you almost forget others are watching your every move and listening to your every word, a three-year-old will always bring it back into perspective. If we regularly model the right way to communicate, forgive, and demonstrate affection, others will notice when something doesn't fit the pattern already established.

Unless you have a prodigy child who loves fruits and vegetables, mealtime can become a battleground in a continual war for peace and health. Around the age of two, kids start asking "why" all day long. One day, Frederick desperately wanted cookies or candy or anything sweet. I gave him a list of healthy options which he quickly denied and he began the "why" assault. After exhausting all other reasons, I finally told him if he ate too much sugar he could get diabetes, which meant he would get poked with a needle everyday for the rest of his life. From that moment on, every time I denied his request for something sweet, he quickly responded with, "Oh yeah, if you eat too much sugary things you get diabetes and get shots every day." If I model a different behavior and binge on junk food, he'll receive mixed signals. Distrust would set in. Whatever we say to those around us, we must back up with our actions.

I could talk all day long about how important it is to show empathy and concern for other people's emotions and well-being, but if I walk right by someone in need or act in an unkind way to people on a regular basis, my kids will learn what a hypocrite looks like rather than a loving and thoughtful individual. I'm sure this type of scrutiny never entered your mind before having kids, but once kids start talking, this reality quickly sets in and they have no problem voicing their honest thoughts, opinions, and feelings.

My three-year-old daughter doesn't want to share anything. It's partially her age, partially her personality. She believes she's justified in taking whatever she wants simply because she wants it. Since generosity is something we place a high value on in our family, we regularly remind her that "we are happy to give." Whenever she grabs something out of someone's hand or throws a tantrum because she can't have something, she typically calms down after hearing that phrase.

To diffuse the situation we assure her that what she is feeling is very real, but sharing and generosity are more important. This means when I'm being selfish about something, both my kids call me out on it. If I want to keep all my birthday chocolate to myself, I am gently and promptly reminded that "we're happy to give." It's in the smallest of moments, actions, and gestures that the deepest beliefs are formed. Let's take those little opportunities and use them well. Let's steward the time we have with the people in our care while they're young so they learn how to steward their own lives as they continue to grow.

opportune timing with kids

You know when you're cooking bacon and there's that perfect moment to pull it out of the pan when it's crispy not burnt, when it's crunchy not chewy? The window of opportunity to create the most delicious piece of bacon passes so quickly. Most of the time we pull the bacon out of the pan too soon fearful it will burn, and then there are those times when we loose focus and end up munching on charred bacon.

With kids most hours of most days are filled with making and consuming food, keeping things sanitary, and maintaining sanity. We don't often get those meaningful deep moments that movies depict. They are as rare as perfectly cooked bacon. It's all about timing and practice.

Rather than forcing moments of opportunity to connect deeply, I find that creating rhythms and space to do low-key activities opens up windows for this to happen naturally. Rituals in your day open up roads to meet on regularly. The meetings may be brief or long depending on the day, but when they can be counted on, those closest to us have a secure space to meet you without distraction or activity.

This will look different depending on the flow of your days and the personalities involved. Carving out 30 minutes of distraction free time everyday produces an open door for connection even if nothing happens most of the time. Try leaving all technology in another room and do something initiated by your child. This consistent connection doesn't have to last hours, but having a chunk of time everyday of undivided attention is so healthy and life giving for your relationship.

This may be a struggle and it may not happen seven days a week, but as you turn it into a habit and it becomes routine, the difficulty diminishes. It becomes just as natural as brushing your teeth and washing your face. Connection must be a normal thing in our days with our kids. Depending on your personality, this will probably be easier for some and harder for others. Give yourself grace and give the process of turning this ritual into a habit the space and time it needs.

I found it very difficult to do this once my kids stopped taking naps. As a natural introvert who requires quiet alone time to recharge everyday, I struggled to have the patience to meet the needs of connection between the lunch hour and dinner hour. Drained of energy and patience, the last thing I desired was undivided attention and connection because I find my energy in my alone time. One day as I was struggling to find a few minutes to myself to think, I realized something powerful: 30 minutes of full attention invested now creates more peace than many hours of partial attention throughout the rest of our day. The same goes for time we spend with anyone. Our full, undivided attention is the greatest gift we can give those around us.

After a week or so of trying this out, it became clear that when they had space to connect without any distractions they were far more content to play on their own for the rest of the day. There are many instances when I fail to do this and guilt sets in, which is when the "good enough" principle must kick in. We must be content in our efforts and confident enough in ourselves to look at what we've attempted and say, "That's good enough." Perfection is never the goal; it doesn't exist anyway so do the best you can with the time and energy you have. When you let the "good enough" principle begin to do its work you'll find you can apply it to other areas of life as well.

face time

Whether we love technology or not, it's here to stay. Phones, screens, and social media are all part of our lives. They represent a major way we stay connected to friends and family. Figuring out how to use these amazing tools is a personal challenge for every individual. The amount and the way we use them must come from an inner conviction rather than an external one. Our kids are part of a generation who will never know what it was like to walk around without a phone. Their lives are posted on social media before they even talk.

I struggled to get a grasp on what was an appropriate amount of time spent on social media for the early years. It was easy access to another world, an escape. One day, my three-year-old son started grabbing at my phone as I texted a friend. He jumped all over me and started making the loudest sounds to get my attention. It dawned on me in that moment that he was missing out on actual, real life face time with me because of the virtual, social time I was spending with my friends. If my days were spent continually glued to my phone and I ignored the faces right in front of me, what was being lost? I had to ask myself this question.

Because we all have different experiences and interactions with technology, we must figure out what healthy use looks like for our own lives. There are apps and programs that can track how much time you spend using which apps—this can be a healthy place to begin reflecting on what amount of time you are at peace with.

For myself, I love taking photos of our days to capture fleeting moments. This was probably the biggest obstacle for me to overcome. I challenged myself to keep my phone plugged into the wall the entire time I was with my kids during the day with only a few exceptions. The small act of keeping it in one location works for me. I'm more attentive to the moment I'm in and when it's quiet time, I pull it out and connect. Know the season you're in. Be mindful and intentional with technology. Give yourself grace to be at peace with how and what you decide to do with the omnipresence of technology.

One-on-one, real life face time with our children, spouses, close friends, and family is a beautiful gift. Since we never know who might move away, let's do the best we can to treasure the physical connection we currently have. One day the only face time we get may be through a screen.

7
remember the moment

"But Mary treasured up all these things, pondering them in her heart." (Luke 2:19 ESV)

Maybe I'm jaded, but I hear this verse quoted so often that it's almost lost its meaning to me. Until one day, I read it and it sank in. I realized we choose what to treasure and what to ponder in our hearts. Whatever we remember becomes the story of our lives. Writing snippets of daily life in a journal, on a phone, or in baby books can be a powerful exercise because it documents our personal history. I don't do it all the time, but every so often I record certain events for wedding days, graduations, or storytelling during future dinners.

One day, Edith decided she would help herself to the box of Cheerios in the cupboard. Unaware she even had the know-how or skills to do such a thing, I blissfully folded laundry in the other room believing she was content and playing with the puzzles we started. Suddenly, I heard a little voice say "uh-oh" accompanied by a couple hundred pitter-patters of rounded oats hitting the kitchen floor. Walking into the room, I realized the reaction and the way I saw this situation determined the story that would be told in the future. Would I let out a huge sigh and begin mumbling complaints under my breath about having to constantly clean up? Would I sharply scold my one and a half year old for independently seeking nourishment? Would I crumple to the floor in exhaustion and let out a little sob? Or would I laugh and ask Edith what happened and wait to see her response?

This verse sprang to the front of my attention as I walked in and laughed at the little girl surrounded by a massive pile of Cheerios gazing up in pure self-satisfaction. The thing I wanted to remember and the story I wanted to tell was of a tenacious little girl who successfully foraged for food, and a mom who laughed and then taught her best way to dig into the Cheerios if she was ever starving for a snack again.

As role models to young believers, mentors to young professionals, and especially parents to young children, we have a hundred or more opportunities a day to write the story of our lives. Some days the tantrums and stubborn refusals to listen can become overwhelming, and I fail to react well. Some days physical and mental exhaustion take over, and in our sleep deprived states we struggle to say a cohesive sentence. There are moments when I immediately regret my reaction, tone, or response. Rather than dwelling on the negative, I remind myself to turn a new page and begin writing a fresh story.

Most of the time in my world, it means snapping a photo that only family members will see. Or maybe sending it to the email account I set up for each of our kids with a little caption. It only happens about once a month, but it's one of the ways I document our days and ponder the stories.

real emotion

The older my kids get the more I realize the depth and range of their emotional lives. What looks like an irrational meltdown to me is a legitimate reaction from a teething toddler who spent most of the night tossing and turning and now wants milk in a pink cup, not a purple cup. Yesterday, she liked purple. Today, she prefers pink. Silly me.

One afternoon I had a list of errands to run so I prepped both kids for our outing. Frederick adamantly refused to go.

He spent the morning in preschool and wanted to cozy up at home playing in his pajamas (or underwear) for the rest of the day. I continued to insist that what I needed to do was important and necessary. This quickly spiraled downward as Frederick protested putting on clothes, socks, and shoes. He was legitimately upset. In that moment of real, raw emotion, it dawned on me that even though I had all the power to force him into the car, it probably wasn't the right decision. There are some days when it is the right thing to do, and I fully believe in teaching our kids how to do things they don't want to do with a good attitude. This moment was not the occasion to flex my all-powerful parenting muscles. It was the time to embrace the very honest and real emotions of my son and pause for the afternoon to meet his need for downtime.

Identifying the real emotion of the moment is tricky. It's healthy and good to validate the feelings we have, but learning how to express the intensity of them is a necessary life lesson. Throughout the day, I find myself saying this type of phrase over and over again, "I'm feeling really frustrated/angry/sad/upset right now because…" Once I put it out there, I talk through why I'm feeling that way and then begin to problem solve ways to lift my mood. It's important for our kids to see us experience a whole range of feelings in a healthy way.

My kids express their sadness in two very unique ways. One of them becomes so brokenhearted and disillusioned that they dissolve into a puddle of tears quickly giving up on life. The other becomes angry-sad lashing out and destroying anything in arms reach. Most of the time, I'm at a loss to understand why, which only intensifies the emotions. I'm not an expert or a psychologist, which is probably why I end up laughing before engaging. I laugh because if I don't, the story will quickly become about a tensely wound-up mom overreacting to her kid's meltdown over not being able to eat chocolate or jump into a pile of rocks. These are the moments I want to remember well because they give the full story. If we ignore these chapters, we neglect to value the importance of our valleys and become lopsided, focusing only on the mountain tops.

We learn more about ourselves and the people we care for in the valleys than we do on the mountain tops. Our difficult days are a testament to perseverance, steadfastness, and courage. Once we walk through the trenches of our children's lows, a deeper level of empathy and connection is built. It's in the valleys that we see the power of grace and mercy—grace to keep going even when we can't see and even when we stumble over obstacles. We find the power of mercy to forgive ourselves, our people, and the circumstances that let us down. Grace is a gift. It comes in the smallest of packages sometimes. It's a kind smile from a stranger as you struggle to maintain sanity grocery shopping with kids. It's the dishwasher that hides the piles of dirty dishes. It's the friend who sends a message of encouragement. These gifts of grace come wrapped in unusual and sometimes funny paper—all we have to do is be willing to open them up and be thankful.

Mountain tops are beautiful and epic. They're a metaphor for those moments of earthly perfection and joy that burst with flavor. It's when the kite catches the wind and floats contentedly in the sky. It's when all the kids sleep through the night and wake up bright eyed and happy to be alive. It's those rare and unique times when contentment reigns in everyone's souls. But, so often we're ready to move on. We get to the top of the mountain out of breath, gasping for air, looking around only to ask, "What's next?" Instead, we should throw a blanket down, crack open the food and drink, and savor the view until the ants show up or the wind makes us chilly. Hold onto those moments for as long as they last. Remember them and encapsulate them in your memory for those days when you're walking through a dark valley. Use them to light up a path of hope and to keep moving forward when steps become tough.

still small moments

Wherever we are, whatever we're doing, we can learn to still ourselves for a moment to see miracle in the mundane. Parenthood in any form can become all-consuming, overwhelming, and daunting. We do get moments of glory when everything falls into place, but these are few and far between. What we usually experience is the tug and pull of trying to get our young ones to do something or stop doing something or go somewhere. We lose sight of the big picture, focusing on the frustration of the current situation. Or we lose sight of the little details concentrating on the end goal.

One warm spring afternoon, I planned on walking to the park near our house to soak up the season change. It just so happened that one of my kids did not want to go on a walk and began to whine the second we began moving toward the door. On a mission to enjoy the weather, we began our trek down the road. After an hour of complaining about the wrong footwear, we went walking through the woods and discovered some early apple blossoms. The birds were singing back and forth, the sun splashed in patches across the grass, the breeze softly blew. Even in this most beautiful moment, the footwear problem reigned supreme.

I'm guilty of doing the same thing all the time. God wants us to enjoy the season, the day, the moment and we can't stop complaining, wondering, and asking questions. We focus on a problem that isn't really a problem or, if it is, it's not worth focusing our energy on because it's something we can't fix or change. All God wants from us is to savor His presence and be present. When we do, we find the surprise apple blossoms, instead of dwelling on wearing the wrong shoes.

Sometimes the present is messy and filled with tears, but these days are just as valid and necessary as the ones that are pristine and filled with laughter. We choose the perspective to take on the story of our lives. Our perspective determines the way we engage with our current moment. Putting the best lens on to focus on the right thing makes all the difference; some days require a telescope while others a microscope. It's up to us to choose the best one. When we do this we are able to have peace in the process and be faithful in our field. Our field is full of seeds waiting to be cared for and tended, and when we engage with the current season we are able to give attention to the needs of those plants as they grow and develop.

Don't forget to take care of yourself and rest. It's essential for maintaining a healthy and sustainable pace in the midst of what some call the busiest season of life. When we are full and nourished, this enables us to seize every opportunity and make the most of it while it lasts. The way we tell our story and how we see our days affects how we engage with the present as well as the way we remember our past. We may not be engaging in the most exciting or life-threatening activities in our current season, but we do have the opportunity to make a difference in our corner of the world with the people closest to us. To do this we must consider the still small moments around us as valuable and worthy of our attention and affection. No matter how little your corner of the world is your expression of love determines its value and greatness. If we begin where we are with what we have, the story of our lives will be rich and meaningful. Choose to embrace the present without regret or longing for another time. Our faithfulness to love those in our field deeply and widely will always produce a beautiful harvest.

about the author

April Best lives in Holland, Michigan with her husband Josh and their two young children. Armed with a Master of Arts in English, she has made her way as a high school French teacher, a middle school English teacher, a book editor, and an author of bible school curriculum. She and her husband are campus leaders at The Point Church in Holland and are currently expecting their third child.

global giving initiative

In pursuit of our mission to help people get their voices and ideas out into the world, we realize that others are concerned with more pressing needs. Finding creativity in every person is important work, but getting food, shelter, and dignity to individuals must come first. That's why Unprecedented Press donates a portion of book revenue to the Everyone Gobal Giving Initative whose goal is to meet the practical needs of individuals around the world and to share the love of Jesus. To learn more, visit *everyoneglobal.com*.

Other titles from
Unprecedented Press

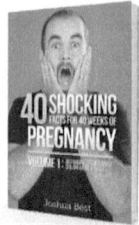

40 Shocking Facts for 40 Weeks of Pregnancy - Volume 1:
Disturbing Details about Childbearing & Birth

By Joshua Best

40 Shocking Facts for 40 Weeks of Pregnancy - Volume 2:
Terrifying Truths about Babies & Breastfeeding

By Joshua Best

She Can Laugh
A Guide to Living Spiritually, Emotionally & Physically Healthy

By Melissa Lea Hughes

Once Upon A Year
Experience a year in the life of Finn

By Joanna Lenau

Y - Christian Millennial Manifesto
*Addressing Our Strengths and Weaknesses
to Advance the Kingdom of God*

Y, The Workbook
A Companion

By Joshua Best

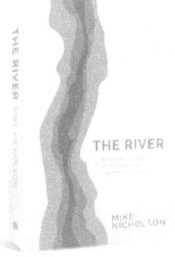

The River
*A 30-day Study on the Role of
the Holy Spirit in the Church,
the World and you*

By Mike Nicholson

Crumbs
100 Everyday Stories about 100 People
By Rose White

Unstuck
*How to Grieve Well and
Find New Footing*

By Danette Johnson

All titles available from Amazon
or from unprecedentedpress.com/shop

www.ingramcontent.com/pod-product-compliance
Lightning Source LLC
Chambersburg PA
CBHW020619300426
44113CB00007B/702